CHARACTERISTICS
OF A CHRISTIAN WOMAN

*A Focus on the Characteristics Portrayed
by a Woman Following after God*

With Love,

Tina

Matthew 6:33

TINA WANAMAKER

That I May
Know Him
PRESS

Printed in the United States of America
First Printing 2021
First Edition 2021

10 9 8 7 6 5 4 3 2 1

All Scripture quotations, unless otherwise indicated, are taken from the
Holy Bible, New King James Version.

CHARACTERISTICS
OF A CHRISTIAN WOMAN

I would like to dedicate this book to Owen.
You are my best friend.

"The Spirit of God has enabled Tina to take the jewels of wisdom from her life experience and pass them on in written form. Her words reflect a humble lover of Christ and a tender listener to His voice. This book is a powerful tool for women to use in a variety of discipleship settings. Read it, share it, apply it, and become a woman of God!"

—Cindy Romberg, pastor's wife, Yakima Missionary Alliance Church, Yakima, Washington

"This is not another 'self-help' book focused on the how-to and not-to-do tips on Christian living. This is a Jesus-help-me book with the primary focus on God's Word, His promises, and His power to help us do His perfect will. With a gentle 'let us get down to the *business* of living a Christ-centered life' approach, the contents of this book evoke the introspection of our spiritual state and call us to immediate obedience to God's Word alone."

—Abby Gordon, business manager of Ecola Bible School, Cannon Beach, Oregon

"'Narrow is the gate.' If you think how we live this life matters and are interested in truth, then you will want to read this beautifully written book. Tina has listened carefully to the voice of the precious Holy Spirit and filled these pages with truth to live by…God's truth. You will learn through these anointed words how every relationship can and should be incredibly wonderful, and exactly what success looks like when lived out according to God's word. Every gold nugget found here will be life changing and prepare you for eternity!"

—Nancy Clayton, family shelter assistant director, Union Gospel Mission

"God has molded and made a beautiful and Spirit-led woman in Tina Wanamaker. I wish I had read this book early in my marriage, motherhood, and walk with the Lord! But this book is needed at any age. It is a great tool for an individual, for mentoring, or group study. Thank you, Tina, for your obedience to the Lord in writing this book!"

—Phyllis Anderson, chaplain, Yakima County Jail

"As a Christian woman, are you desiring to lead a life of excellence for the glory of God? Tina will openly and pragmatically walk you through the needed characteristics of loving God, husband, children, and friends. This book will lead your heart, soul, and spirit to Jesus—the One who is able to do beyond all we can ask or imagine (see Ephesians 3:20). If your life is in need of transformation or you desire to have a transforming influence on others, this is your guide!

—Mary Forsman, wife, homeschooling mom of five, staff member of the Flying H Youth Ranch

TABLE OF CONTENTS

Acknowledgments 1

Introduction 3

Chapter 1 7

A Christian Woman Is Loving

Chapter 2 17

Love Made Practical

Chapter 3 29

Loving Our Children

Chapter 4 39

Practically Loving Our Children

Chapter 5 51

Christian Friendship

Chapter 6 67

Graciousness in Offenses

Chapter 7 79

Practical Graciousness in Offense

About the Author 97

Other Works from the Author

Acknowledgments

I would like to take a moment to acknowledge that Jesus Christ is my Lord and Savior. He is, He was, and He will be forevermore. He has brought me out of a place of darkness and conveyed me into the light of the kingdom of His love. God has set my feet upon a Rock that is higher than I. He is everything. He is my life. Thank you, Father, for all You have done. Jesus, You say that if we acknowledge You before men that You will acknowledge us before the Father. May You be glorified!

I would also like to take a moment to acknowledge some sweet people the Lord has brought into my life. First and foremost, my husband, Owen. He is a precious gem! What a wonderful man the Lord has provided for a husband. I am beyond thankful. My sweet children, Levi, Sabille, Addison, and Ira. They are gifts from God. My mom, who is always supportive. My dad, who has demonstrated a portion of God's love to me. And my siblings, their spouses, and children, whom I love dearly. Also Owen's parents, whom I am so thankful for, as well as his brothers and their families. And then there are those who have prayed for me specifically during the process of this book. You who have engaged in countless discussions, answered countless questions, and have spent time on your knees in prayer. Thank you! I count you each as precious to me! I know beyond a doubt that God has given a good and wonderful gift in each of you! Without you it would just be the worst! (I just had to throw this in for you, my sweet friends!) Thank you all for your enthusiasm! I want you to know that you have part in the fruit of this book. Lisa and Mary, thank you so much for all your support! It has been priceless. Rachel, you are a treasure. After five little ones you are still blessing those around you!

As for Sarah...what would I do without your persistent prayers as well as your friendship? You truly are my sister. I enjoy our fellowship immensely! And thank you to my dear and sweeter-er friend who gave permission for me to use part of her story. I am thankful God brought you to be part of our family! Miss KK, otherwise known as Kayla...I am so thankful for your insight and ever cheerful manner. You are such a blessing to all you meet! Thank you Dori Harrell with Breakout Editing for all your editing. It seems that the way God orchestrated our meeting could be a chapter in and of itself! I am thankful for you, sister. And lastly, but not least, thank you to Abby Gordon, who helped through your photography with cover ideas! God has given a good and precious gift through you (and the hours spent over the years discussing God's word at 5:00 a.m.). I praise the Lord for all of these precious gifts, from family to friends! I just love you all to pieces!

INTRODUCTION

The purpose of writing this small book is to encourage you as a Christian woman to seek the Lord for all your needs. God is more than sufficient to provide what you and I need. He has given us all things pertaining to life and godliness. God has provided everything we need to live a life of holiness and to practically live out His Word on a daily basis. This is not to say that we will not sin, for we understand that all have fallen short of the glory of God. We are sinners saved by grace, which is simply favor from God that we do not deserve. But we are still called to live a life of excellence for the glory of God. Can we do it? Only by God's grace. We will make mistakes, but His grace is enough.

The secondary purpose is simply to do what Titus 2 tells us...that the older women teach the younger. When my husband and I came to Christ, I had no idea of how to practically be a Christian woman. I didn't know how to live out Jesus in my life, marriage, parenting, friendships, or relationships with others. So I asked God to teach me. Jesus tells us in Matthew 11:29, "Take My yoke upon you and learn from Me." He is the best teacher we could ever have. I asked, and He taught. I am happy to share some of what He has taught over the years in the hopes that it may help, encourage, and provide practical examples of what being a Christian woman actually looks like. I am far from perfect. In fact, I am a big sinner…just like you. What God has done in me testifies of how great He is! And if God can do such a huge work in my heart, then He can do it in yours as well! I am confident in the Lord's abilities to change, conform, make new, and just blow our socks off in regard to His working in us!

My desire is not to offend in any way, although we know that Jesus is a rock of offense and that His word may be offensive to some. As a new believer, I found my flesh rebelling against a godly principle that appeared in a book I was reading. I had to put the book down and pick it up a few months later after God had prepared my heart to receive His Word. If you find yourself offended at, or your heart in rebellion to, His Word, take some time to bring that struggle before the Lord and seek His heart in the matter. I encourage you to read Characteristics of a Christian Woman with an open heart and mind. Ask God to prepare your heart to receive from Him. Take from it what God has for you. Allow God to do His work in you. Our Father sometimes asks us to do difficult things. Practically living out His Word can be hard. But it is in the hard things that we learn the most. And it is in the most difficult things that we are the most conformed into the image of Jesus. Our Lord desires us not only to read the Bible, but to do the Bible.

The Bible study that partners with this book is meant to be used in conjunction with the corresponding lesson numbers. Lesson one goes with chapter one. The study lessons follow each chapter. When I taught these topics in our ladies' group, the study guide was passed out first, and then the text was received from the Lord to teach at the weekly meetings. The text became the basis for this publication, although some of this teaching God had led me to write before I taught it to a group as a short six-week study. As it is now, it would be a nine-week study, with week one as the introduction and week nine as a review. I would suggest that if done in a group setting, the study be done the same week the chapter is read, and then the topic be discussed at the weekly meeting. Or just the chapter can be read and discussed. If you're reading this book in your personal time and not for a weekly meeting, use the Bible study as you view the most helpful.

The study lessons may be used on their own as well without the chapter text. If taught in a weekly Bible study setting, I encourage the teacher not to just reiterate what she has read but to really to take time seeking the Lord for what He specifically has for her particular group of ladies. Teachers, your ladies have specific needs, some of which even you may be unaware of. But God always knows. And as you seek Him, He will meet those needs through your efforts. Never be afraid to present God's Word. Although some of these topics may be difficult to discuss with ladies, never shrink back from the Word. The topics in His Word that bring us the most discomfort are more than likely the very things we need to study!

The study guide was designed to help you begin to think about the subject and God's Word pertaining to it before discussing it in a group setting. It is not meant to be an end within itself but merely a starting point for a deeper discussion. It is likely that God will speak to you further regarding these issues. Continue conversing with the Lord in these matters. These topics will hold lifelong learning opportunities for us as ladies. We shall never "arrive" in an area, but we shall see much growth—if we allow God room to work and let Him teach us.

My prayer is that after reading this small endeavor at pointing you to Christ Jesus, that you will feel equipped to embark on a closer walk with Him. That you would be inspired to take the next step in your relationship with our Lord. That you will feel challenged in your walk with Him! May you take God at His word and step out in faith in obedience to it! And then may you experience the blessing of obedience to God's Word!

CHAPTER 1

A CHRISTIAN WOMAN IS LOVING

As Christian women we are to love one another. The hallmark of a Christian woman should be love. John tells us in 1 John 4:7, "Beloved, let us love one another." We should show love in word, action, and attitude. But before this love can be shared with the world around us, it must be practically lived out in our homes. This means that we love those in our homes first. We cannot minister or love effectively outside the home if this love is not first practiced by us within the home. We cannot demonstrate what we have not experienced or act out what we don't know on a personal level. We must know this love on a heart level and not just an intellectual level. An outward demonstration of Christ's love begins with an inward realization of this love toward ourselves. The inner working of God's love within our hearts naturally flows to others. It is an inner work being shown outwardly.

Loving others must start within us as we recognize God's love overflowing in our own hearts. Romans 5:5 tells us that "the love of God has been poured out in our hearts by the Holy Spirit who was given to us." We must first experience the love of God toward us before we can begin to show this love toward others. Let's think of our hearts as a hearth. Before we are in relationship with Christ, we have cold and unlit logs on the hearth. There is no warmth, no radiance, and no light. All is cold and dark. When the understanding of His love for us dawns within our hearts, it is like a small flame has been lit.

As our comprehension deepens and we believe by faith in His love for us, that small flame is fanned into a fire. Now there is warmth, the radiance of Christ, and light emanating from the hearth of our hearts. This fire of God's love on the hearth of our hearts lights the path for others to come to an understanding of His love for them. If we do not have the fire of God's love burning within, we will be unable to light the path for another. We can only explain what we have understanding of. We can then begin to demonstrate and verbalize the love that was demonstrated toward us.

How was God's love demonstrated toward us? Romans 5:8 says, "But God demonstrated His own love toward us, in that while we were still sinners, Christ died for us." God showed the depth and power of His love for us in that while we were still dead in our sins, Christ died for us. This is a sacrificial love. It is all encompassing. No more love could be shown than what God showed by giving us His Son to die for our sins. This is the fuel for the fire that is lit on the hearth of our hearts. And our sin is what is burned up in that fire of pure and sacrificial love. How can we, who have experienced God's great love, even begin to put this love into words? Our efforts will fall short by far, but we shall try.

Take a moment to stop and think of all the sins committed in your life. All the selfishness, all the pride, debauchery perhaps, lifestyles best left unspoken. All of this Christ Jesus died for—while we were yet sinners, Christ died for us. Now take all this accumulated sin from one life and multiply it by all the people on the planet today. Then take that sin and multiply it by all the people who have ever lived throughout history. Ultimately you end up with a gigantic wasteland of sin. Piles upon piles, stacks upon stacks, and mountains upon mountains of sin. This is the sin that Jesus died for. This is the love God demonstrated toward us.

When we think in terms of the vastness of sin accumulated over time, we begin to see the vastness of the ocean of God's love for us. Romans 5:8 takes on new meaning. Jesus died for all sin— the stacks, piles, and mountains—but also for us individually. Let's make it more personal. Add your name in the blank. "But God demonstrates His own love toward you, _____, in that while you, _____, were still a sinner, Christ died for you." It is only as we understand this truth of God's great love for us that we can begin to demonstrate this love to others.

If you do not understand the great love God has for you, then simply ask Him to reveal it to you. Ask Him to light that fire or fan the flames on the hearth of your heart. One way to gain a greater understanding is to begin a search through the Scriptures for verses pertaining to God's love. Use the concordance in the back of your Bible or another concordance to find them. Write the verses out. Once you have done this, simply ask God to show you His great love for you on a personal level. Ask Him to speak to you through His Word. God is faithful and will answer. He will begin to show you His great love for you.

The grasping of God's great love for you will never be completed. Our human minds will never be able to fully comprehend all that God did specifically for each one of us. We can't understand the depth of suffering Jesus endured. And it goes over our heads to know that Jesus would do it all over again just for you or me. Isaiah 55:8 tells us that God's ways are not our ways and His thoughts are not our thoughts. His love and care for us is so incomprehensible and complete! How wonderful is our God! How mighty is He who has made a way for our sins to be paid for! God has taken the handwriting of requirements out of the way and nailed them to the cross. The price is fully paid. There is no more for us to do but to believe and receive. Praise His name! May we more deeply understand the truth of God's love and experience it on a heart level. We must take God's claim of His love for us by faith and stand upon it. Many times we come to Christ with so much baggage that we just can't believe that God could really love us and that Jesus could really die for us. Believe it! His word is true. He does not lie. His love for you is like the ocean in its vastness. It is so incredibly deep and wide. Trust Him and believe in His love for you!

Once we claim this truth of God's love for us and experience it, then we are called to show this love toward those in our immediate spheres, our homes. We are called to let the fire of love within our hearts burn brightly toward those around us. To let them feel the warmth, see the light it produces, and observe the radiance of Christ through us. When we truly experience God's love, we feel compelled to share! His love is within us, and now we have opportunity to pour it out in our homes.

Why should we start in the home? There are two reasons for this. The first reason is found in Acts 1:8: "But you shall receive power when the Holy Spirit has come upon you; and you shall be witnesses to Me in Jerusalem, and in all Judea and Samaria, and to the end of the earth." The disciples were to minister at their home base first and then move on to other places. We too should follow the example here in Scripture and minister at our home bases first. It is much harder to practically show love in our homes than to those outside the home. This is because the folks in our homes know us thoroughly. They see us on the good days. They see us on the bad days. They know what we are like when we are sick or irritable or tired. And we are called to love on the good, the bad, the sick, the irritable, and the tired days.

The people outside the home most likely know us more on the good days, when we are put together and have a smile on. The goal is to be that same person to those outside the home as we are to those inside the home. So we need to start in the home first. We need to get in the trenches and get our training in loving done at home before taking it out to others. The progression of God's love goes from our own hearts to those in our homes to those in our spheres of influence to those outside our spheres of influence.

The second reason is simply so that we will not be hypocrites. If we go out to show the love of Christ to others while our homes are in discord due to us not demonstrating Christ's love there, then we are being hypocritical. May I suggest that we stay home and beseech our Lord until we get it right? Our witness for Christ can be destroyed on this one point. If we go out teaching on the love of Christ and that we should love others, but we aren't doing it at home, then we have a discrepancy between our walk and our talk. We must understand that we will all make mistakes, but we need to have an overall attitude of seeking to love in our homes.

James 1:22 says, "But be doers of the Word, and not hearers only, deceiving yourselves." We can't just hear that we should love—we must act on it! 1 John 3:18 tells us, "Let us not love in word or in tongue, but in deed and in truth." We have to do God's love. Loving others must start within us as we experience God's love and then extend that love to those closest to us. Think of those living in your home now. This is your first ministry area. It may be your husband, children, parents, uncle, aunt, or roommate. The home is where we begin to actively live out the love shown us.

We have established that we must initially experience the love of God on a personal level before in turn forwarding it to others. We have discussed the flame of God's love on the hearth of our hearts and that it will give light to others around us. The depth of God's love has been examined and how it applies to us personally. We have also established that this demonstration of love begins on the home front toward whomever we live with and then moves outward in our spheres of influence. We naturally must now move to a practical application of love. We will discuss how to love on a daily basis in the next chapter.

LESSON 1 STUDY QUESTIONS

Loving Begins in Our Homes

A Christian woman loves others. Seeing that this love must begin in our homes, we begin with those closest to us...our husbands. Titus 2:4 exhorts or encourages the older women "that they admonish the young women to love their husbands." We as wives know that we should love our husbands. But what does this look like in day-to-day living? What are some practical examples of showing this love to our husbands? Take some time before you begin studying this to ask God to reveal any areas you could improve upon...and that He would cause you to be a doer of the Word and not a hearer only!

1. What do you think it means to practically show love to your husband?

2. Look up the following verses or chapters. Record what each verse or section tells us about loving.

   a) 1 Corinthians 13

   b) Proverbs 10:12

3. Do the verses above change your view on how you should love your husband? If so, how?

4. Has the Lord shown you any areas you could improve upon in showing love to your husband? What are they?

5.   What can you do differently to change the things God has revealed?

Romans 12:9 says, "Let love be without hypocrisy." May we learn to love our husbands as the Lord desires so that we may not live a hypocritical life. Loving others must first start in our own homes. Only then can it be poured forth to others.

_____

_____

_____

_____

_____

_____

_____

_____

_____

_____

_____

_____

_____

_____

_____

_____

_____

Study Notes

CHAPTER 2

LOVE MADE PRACTICAL
Loving Our Husbands

What does this love practically look like in our homes? How do we live out the love of Christ in our families? Titus 2:3–4 says, "The older women likewise, that they be reverent in behavior...not given to much wine, teachers of good things—that they admonish the young women to love their husbands, to love their children." Here Paul is telling Titus to remind the older women of their obligation to caution the younger women to love their husbands and children. Apparently the older women have already learned to love their husbands and children and are now commanded to admonish, or gently reprove, the younger women to do so as well. This does not mean that once the older women learn to love their families that they stop doing it. They must continue in loving them even as they are admonishing others to do so. Their example of loving will seal the deal in the younger women following after them. May I suggest that it would be difficult to receive advice from another woman regarding this issue if she was not living this love out in her own life? We gain credibility in sharing what we have learned as we actively live it out in our lives. And so, older and younger women are both to love their husbands and children.

How do we do it? Let's look first at loving our husbands. The Greek word for love used in "love their husbands" in Titus 2:4 is philandros. It means to show affection, fondness, or friendliness toward your husband. The idea is that we express a strong and tender attachment to our husbands. That we are favorably inclined toward them—we want the best for them and are willing and happy to help achieve this, either through our actions or supporting them in their vision for life. That we cherish kind regard for them and strongly prefer them over others. Basically, that we are nice to them, have kind feelings for them, support them, and let them know that we prefer their company over any other.

You may be asking, what if they don't deserve my kindness and tenderness? Let me be plain—it does not matter if they deserve it or not. Give it to them anyway. God's Word doesn't say that the women should love their husbands only if they are worthy. Did you or I deserve mercy for our sins? Were we worthy of Christ's death for us? No...but we still received it freely. And this unmerited favor that we received from our Lord changed us completely. It is still changing us. What is to say that your unmerited favor toward your husband won't cause change in him? It is God's goodness and kindness that leads to repentance. And it only makes sense that our goodness and kindness toward our husbands would bring the same response.

This idea goes along with the next question: What if he is not a Christian? 1 Peter 3:1–2 says, "Wives, likewise, be submissive to your own husbands, that even if some do not obey the Word, they, without a word, may be won by the conduct of their wives, when they observe your chaste conduct accompanied by fear." Wives can win their unbelieving husbands to the Lord by their godly manner, without preaching at them. The husband's behavior can be changed as the wife shows him affection and unmerited favor. And so, if he is not a believer in Christ Jesus, you may open his heart to salvation through your conduct in Christ by loving him. Show him kindness and affection and see what the Lord will do. Believe the promises in the Bible! There are countless stories of women taking the Word of God at face value, believing it, living it out, and seeing their husbands come to Jesus or draw closer to Him.

This principle found in 1 Peter does not only apply to unbelieving husbands, but believing husbands as well. How often do we as wives find ourselves desiring to see change in our husbands! Over and over I have heard the same thing from women regarding their husbands. They want them to be leaders in the home, to be better fathers, more considerate, closer to the Lord, and so on. These desires can be realized only as we are obedient to the Bible.

As we live out the Word on a consistent basis, we will begin to see changes in our husbands. The Lord begins to mold and change them. This is a direct result of us being doers of the word in this area of submitting to God and loving our husbands. There is no promise for the husband to see his wife change...the promise is for the wife to see the husband change. But we must take the first step! Do not waste your time any longer on wishing things would be different, getting upset about your situation, or spinning your wheels trying to effect change. It's time to move on from there. Just believe the Word of God and do it!

The last question that comes to mind is, what if I don't feel like being affectionate toward my husband? Simple...once again, just do it anyway! In our house, we tell our children, "We don't go by our feelings. We go by the Word of God." Many times I have had to take this advice myself. As you step out in obedience to the Lord, He will give you feelings of affection toward your husband. Ask Him to provide you the feelings of affection for your husband if you are lacking them. Matthew 7:7 tells us that if we ask, we shall receive. Of course, we must ask in accordance with God's will. And showing love or affection toward your husband is in accordance with His will, so we know that He will provide the means...and the feelings to do so. I am speaking from experience in this area.

My husband and I accepted Jesus as our Savior after we were married a little over a year. I was completely clueless as to how to be a Christian woman, let alone a Christian wife. About two years after we gave our lives to Christ, the Lord really began to convict me through His Word on my role as a wife. I realized many things during this time, and the Lord began an overhaul in my heart. One of the first things was that I was not honoring my husband. Ephesians 5:33 says, "And let the wife see that she respects her husband." The word in Greek for respect means literally to be in awe of. The idea is that a wife should respect her husband's position in the home and in return that he should respect hers. That we give honor where honor is due.

The problem was that I had some feminist ideas (not feminine) and didn't want to honor him. But I desired to be obedient to my Father in heaven and so stepped out in obedience to His Word. It was difficult, and I didn't know exactly how to honor my husband. But the Lord blessed my desire to be obedient with a changed heart and taught me how to honor Owen. God provided opportunities to honor Him by honoring my husband.

Let me give an example of how this worked on a practical level. I had not been allowing my husband to make larger decisions in our home. I realized that I needed to let him be the man. I needed to show him respect and honor by letting him lead. God showed me through His word and taught me, and then I began asking for opportunities to honor him. For occasions to put it into practice. And God provided! We needed to purchase a vehicle. Owen told me that he had found a car he felt would work for us. I felt the Lord showing me this was an opportunity to honor my husband. I felt I should not even go and look at the vehicle but rather just let Owen lead. I put my trust in the Lord and surrendered the situation and car purchase to Him. I realized that even if it was the wrong decision, God would bless my obedience to Him. My husband was able to buy a car with full support from me in whatever the outcome was.

That was huge for me. It dealt with finances, trust in God, and surrender on my part of the decision making. The Lord walked with me through this process and allowed me to show honor to my husband in this. And to this day the opportunities to respect and honor Owen have not ceased. The more I stepped out in obedience to the Lord and His Word in this, the easier it became. And then I actually began to want to honor my husband! Talk about a changed heart! As we step out in obedience to our Lord, He will align our hearts with His will. Amazing! If the Lord can change my stubborn heart, then I am quite sure He can change yours! Just as the Lord changed my heart in regard to honoring my husband, He can change yours in regard to showing affection, if it is needed. Now that we know it can be practically done with the Lord's help, let's look at how to do it.

What are some ways we can show loving affection or favorable inclination toward our husbands? Showing this loving affection or favorable inclination is an outward demonstration of the inner change Christ has wrought within our hearts. As we discussed in chapter one, it is allowing that fire of God's love on the hearth of our hearts to burn brightly and exhibit warmth and light to our husbands, in this case through loving affection and favorable inclination.

How does a wife practically show that she is favorably inclined toward her husband? Basically, we need to be kind and thoughtful. It sounds simple, and it is! A few ideas: get up and refill his coffee cup without being asked, give him a shoulder rub, hold his hand, bring him the newspaper, make him his favorite dinner, help him do a chore, encourage him through your words, tell him you think he is great, compliment him, and build him up. Every man is different and will respond to different loving and affectionate actions. Ask the Lord to reveal specific opportunities to show love to your husband. Remember Matthew 7:7. The Lord will give ideas if you ask Him, because this is His will for you.

Let me just say that we are not showing loving kindness through service because we are less than our husbands. It seems some have the mindset that because a wife is called to demonstrate love and service to her husband, she is less than him. This was where I was at when Owen and I first married. I would not serve him because I wanted to show that I was not beneath him. In a healthy marriage, the husband and wife serve one another, although sometimes in different ways. The husband and wife have distinct roles and positions within the home. When both are moving within the parameters set for them in God's Word, it is a beautiful thing.

We are created as equals with our husbands. The wife is called to submit to the authority of the husband. The husband is called to love the wife as Christ loves the church. I would say the husband definitely has the harder part! We are God's creation, just as our husbands are. But there must be an authority in the home. Otherwise, confusion ensues. Think of a home like a company. If there were two bosses, who would you take orders from? Which one would make the decisions? Who would the employees listen to? I have seen this play out with a friend in his workplace. One boss would tell him to do something, and then the other would say not to do it. Confusing! God is a God of order. He does not work in confusion. So it makes sense to place someone in charge in the home so this kind of thing does not occur.

The husband is the head of the house. He is in authority over his household. The wife is not any less than her husband—she is just in a different position than him. She still has opinions, desires, and motivations. Placing yourself under your husband's authority in the home does not make you any less of a woman. In all actuality, it makes you more of a woman. A woman who takes God's Word seriously and desires to live it out. A woman who is under submission to God first and then her husband. A woman who desires to have her marriage be an example of God's love, mercy, and grace. God has a wonderful plan in regard to marriage, and as we follow the instructions given through His Word, we get to see this played out in our lives!

There are situations in a marriage that void submitting to your husband at that specific time. If your husband asks you to commit a crime, do not submit. If your husband asks you to do something that goes against God's Word, do not submit. For example, if your husband asked you to help him plan a bank heist, you would not submit to that. God's Word clearly states we should not steal. Not only that, but it is illegal. Ladies, make sure that what he is asking you to do is sin before you take your stance. Do not refuse to submit just because you don't want to do something he wants to do. Do not claim that what he is desiring is going against God's Word without doing the research and making sure it is. This is a strong stance to take, so make sure that you are sure before refusing. And make sure you have spent time seeking God and His will in the matter.

As we discussed earlier, if we ask according to God's will, then He will answer us. He will give us the specifics that we need. He will supply all we need to love our husbands. The essence of demonstrating love to our husbands is service. How can we love them? We can serve them. We can esteem them higher than ourselves, as Philippians 2:3 puts it. If we are living out this kind of love in our home, then as we share this love with others, it will be done in humility and sincerity. We will have the true understanding that loving our husbands is sacrificial and requires humbling ourselves before our God. Don't make the mistake of thinking sacrifice and humility are bad things. Sacrifice and humility are what Jesus taught us through the example of His life.

Loving our husbands and children in this way will require us to stay in this place of sacrifice and humility. Why? Because we will not always want to love them the way we are called to and will need to humble our hearts and sacrifice our will in order to do so. We will be called to submit our will to God's will.

Remember that obedience to God and His Word will yield a blessing. Hebrews 10:36 tells us, "For you have need of endurance, so that after you have done the will of God, you may receive the promise." After we have done the will of God, we shall receive His promise! We shall receive His promise of rest, peace, joy, or whatever He chooses to bestow upon us. We have need of endurance, that we may obtain God's promise after we have been obedient to Him. If you are already living this obedience out, keep it up! Wait for the promise! If you are just beginning your journey of loving your husband, dive on in! God is faithful and will provide all you need!

LESSON 2 STUDY QUESTIONS

Submission to Husbands

A Christian woman is submissive to her own husband. The Bible tells us many times to submit to our husbands. But what does the word submit mean? How does submission play out on a practical level? And why would we want to submit to our husbands? Let's find out! The Bible has all the answers we need!

1.   Describe what you think submitting to your husband means.

2.   Look up the following verses. Record what each verse tells us about submitting.

   a) Titus 2:5

   b) 1 Peter 3:1

   c) Ephesians 5:22

3.   Do the verses above change your view on submitting to your husband?

4.   What is the benefit of submission to your husband?

Study Notes

_____

_____

_____

_____

_____

_____

_____

_____

_____

_____

_____

_____

_____

_____

_____

_____

_____

_____

_____

_____

_____

_____

_____

CHAPTER 3

N ow we move on to looking at loving our children. Let us revisit a portion of Titus 2:4 again: "That they admonish the young women to love their husbands, to love their children." The Greek word used here for loving our children is philoteknos. It means a maternal love or fondness for your children. This is the idea that we are to love our children, to regard them with pleasure and tenderness, and to strongly prefer them over others. It means we are to have tender feelings for them, that we like to be around them, and we enjoy them.

The older women were told to admonish (to encourage, advise) the younger women to love their husbands and children. Shouldn't loving our husbands and children come naturally to us as women? As soon as your child is born, don't you automatically love and enjoy her or him? To a degree we do. But fast-forward a few months to the point where we haven't slept in what seems like ages, have changed so many diapers we have lost count, and our sweet husbands don't understand why we are upset when they aren't helping with the baby...then we need that admonishment. At that time we must choose to love our families. We don't always have the feelings of tenderness, but we always have the choice to obey God's Word.

If you were not raised in a Christian home where maternal tenderness was shown and pleasure was associated with the children, then you may not know how to show it to your children. But God is always faithful to supply all that we need pertaining to life and godliness. He will teach you! The many times I have come to God in these areas are countless! And each time, He has proved faithful. If you ask God to teach you to be the mother that He desires, He will teach you! If you feel that you have no natural love or fondness for your child or children, God can provide it. God can change our hearts and views regarding our children.

We should not view our children as a burden but as a delight. We must constantly renew our minds with the fact that our children are a gift. Psalm 127:3 tells us, "Behold, children are a heritage from the Lord, The fruit of the womb is a reward." And again in Psalm 127:5 it says, "Happy is the man who has his quiver full of them." Children are a blessing from God. This goes against everything that our culture tells us, thus necessitating a constant renewal of our minds in the fact that our children are a blessing. Our culture today sends a message that our children are a bother to us. We are told we should only have a certain number of them. That they should be seen and not heard. Children are not seen as

God sees them but as a busy world does. God views children as precious in His sight. We remember Jesus telling His disciples to let the little children come to Him in Matthew 19. As this barrage of messages from the world comes our way, we must weigh them against the Bible and find what is true and then reject the false.

For a while, every time a thought entered my mind that my children were a burden, I would say aloud, "My children are a blessing!" I constantly battled these thoughts from the world with God's Word and His perspective toward my children. And after a while, I realized they actually were a blessing. But as noted before, it is a constant renewal. Even now I must remind myself that these children are given as a gift to my husband and me. God is continuing this process of renewing my mind in regard to my children. He has done a lot of work in me, but there is still much to do. We must use Scripture to battle worldly thoughts about our families.

When we desire the attention of our Father in heaven, He is never annoyed or burdened by us. We come to Him, and we know we are accepted and loved. We don't come expecting God to say, "Oh, here she is again with another question!" We know that God the Father delights in us and we in Him. He doesn't mind our questions. He is not bothered by our constant coming to Him. Our pattern for parenting comes from the perfect pattern we see demonstrated between our heavenly Father and His children. God the Father regards us with tenderness. He knows our frames, that we are but dust, and deals gently with us according to His great loving-kindness. He takes pleasure in us. He enjoys us. Let me say that again…God takes pleasure in you! He desires you to come to Him and spend time with Him. He enjoys your presence!

And because our pattern for parenting comes from our relationship with our Father in heaven, we should take our cues from that relationship. We should not be annoyed by yet more questions from our children. God has created our children with this innate curiosity. Shall we be annoyed by what God has placed within them? We should not be burdened when our children want to crawl up on our laps just to spend time with us. The children will one day be grown and out of our care—may we put the task aside and enjoy each child and the moment God has provided.

Let us now apply these things to our relationship with our children. Do we view them as a burden or a delight? Are we annoyed when our children ask us questions, or do we enjoy the personal time with them? Do we show them harshness or tenderness? Do we have a strong preference for our children? Would we rather be with our husbands and children than with anyone else?

If you are not following God's pattern for parenting, which He lays out in His word and by His example with us, do not despair! Do not condemn yourself! As Romans 8:1 says, "There is therefore now no condemnation to those who are in Christ Jesus." We are all a work in progress. We are all sinners in need of a Savior.

We cannot change our ways if we do not first see a need for it. God sets a standard for us and shows this to us through the Bible. When we realize that we are falling short of what He is asking of us, then we employ 1 John 1:9: "If we confess our sins, He is faithful and just to forgive us our sins and to cleanse us from all unrighteousness." As we confess our unloving attitudes, harshness, or lack of interest in our children, we are forgiven and cleansed from all unrighteousness. As Isaiah 1:18 tells us, "Though your sins are like scarlet, they shall be white as snow; Though they are red like crimson, They shall be as wool."

We are fully forgiven and fully cleansed. It is like we have a white board that we have made ugly black marks all over. The board is us—it is our hearts, our days. The ugly marks are our sins. When we repent or ask forgiveness, it is as if God takes the white board eraser and erases all our sins. Then He uses the board cleaner to clean any underlying marks. It is fully cleansed, in pristine condition. We have a fresh start. What will we write now? Will we once again make ugly marks with harsh words to our children? Or will we instead create a beautiful picture with words of love and encouragement to them?

Once again, do not condemn yourself when you fail. And you will fail, just as I will. But rather repeat the process found in 1 John as often as needed. In conjunction with repentance, ask God to teach you how to be the mother He desires. Ask Him to teach you how to love your children. Ask God to renew your mind toward them. As described in the prior chapter, He is faithful to do this for you. God will teach you how to love your children and what it means to love them, if you ask Him.

What does it mean to have a maternal love or fondness for your children? Maternal love is a motherly love. This is the natural love God gives a mother for her children. It is the desire to nurture, protect, and guide your child. As well as these things, maternal love includes fondness for your children. Maternal love is God given, but it may be quenched by circumstance, example, drug use, or other things.

Once again, we may not have had this maternal love or fondness modeled to us in our homes when we were growing up. We may not have had an example to learn from. Even now, we may not see this maternal love toward children around us in others. Hopefully there is a Christ-following mother we can look to as a practical example. But even if there is not, there is still hope that we can learn this. We have seen that we learn these things as we ask God to train us, ask Him to put love or fondness in our hearts for our children, and simply sit at the feet of Jesus and receive from Him.

If there is a human example of maternal love and fondness for children in your life, then take time to glean from her how she learned and put these characteristics into practice. Always be sure that the lady you are seeking advice from is in the Word and living it out. It is okay to ask questions of her to determine this before sharing your heart with her. A woman truly following Jesus will not mind these questions, and in all actuality she will appreciate your desire to make sure you are receiving godly counsel. These ladies can be a good resource for us as we seek and learn how to be the mother God desires us to be. But make sure that you do not seek their advice first. Our first avenue for learning about mothering is the Lord. Seek God first. Ask Him to provide maternal love and fondness in your heart for your children. He always comes through!

CHAPTER 3 STUDY QUESTIONS

Loving Our Children

A Christian woman loves her children. She has a tender heart toward them and seeks their highest good. Wisdom tells us that our children begin to define their relationship with God through their relationship with their parents. The mother is usually the one who has the most contact with the children. Therefore it is only logical that the tone of the mother sets the tone of the children. If the mother is tender, gentle, kind, and firm with the children, then the children pick that up. The mother and child relationship was designed to be one of love. Unfortunately, many homes are broken, and this love relationship is not shown. But God, in His infinite mercy, can and will teach us what this relationship should look like. We will look at what the Bible tells us about a loving relationship with our children and also discover how this is lived out daily.

1.   What do you think it means to love your children?

2.   Look up the following verses and write them out. Make a note of what each verse says about loving.

   a) John 13:34

   b) 1 Peter 4:8

   c) Colossians 3:14

3.   How can we practically show our children love?

4.   Titus 2:4 brings us back to the older women admonishing the younger women to love their children. The word for love in this verse carries the meaning of a maternal love, fondness for, and enjoyment of our children. How can we show fondness for our children?

5.   What does it mean to enjoy them and what does that look like?

_____

_____

_____

_____

_____

_____

_____

_____

_____

_____

_____

_____

_____

_____

Study Notes

_____

_____

_____

_____

_____

_____

_____

_____

_____

_____

_____

_____

_____

_____

_____

_____

_____

_____

_____

_____

_____

_____

_____

CHAPTER 4

PRACTICALLY LOVING OUR CHILDREN

A Christian woman loves her children not in word only, but also in deed. She practically lives out loving her children on a daily basis. What does this look like? How do you practically love your children? How can you demonstrate the fondness we discussed in chapter three? What does it actually look like to take pleasure in them? I would venture to say that many women today do not know how to truly love their children. We no longer see a pattern of maternal love before us. All around us we are faced with messages that urge us to be self-centered instead of others centered. When we are self-focused, we will never be content as mothers. We will be constantly looking to fulfill our own needs and desires instead of filling those of our families. We must be God focused. When our focus is upon God first, then our husbands, and then our children, we begin to find true contentment.

True contentment is found in fulfilling God's calling for our lives. The essence of motherhood is service. Matthew 20:28 tells us that Jesus came to serve and not to be served. Once we have received Christ Jesus as our Savior, then His Spirit dwells within us. This is a Spirit of service. The Holy Spirit serves in many ways. He teaches, rebukes, convicts, brings Scripture to mind as we need it, conforms us into the image of Christ, and leads us. So, we have a Spirit of service within us. And we are also being conformed into the image of the One who came not to be served, but to serve. Because of this we can only find true contentment in fulfilling the prompting and calling to serve. Every follower of Jesus Christ is called to serve. Mothers are called to serve their children, their families. We can find contentment in doing this. Part of the daily loving of our children is our service to them.

Now back to the practical loving of our children. We understand that the foundation of truly loving our children is experiencing the love of Christ. We also understand that a way of expressing this love is through our service to them and that in this we can begin to find contentment. We may practically show fondness for our children by serving them. Of course, our children must be taught to serve others as well. They learn through our example of service to our God, to our husbands, to them, and to others.

As they watch us serve with a cheerful heart, they are learning to serve with cheerful hearts. Conversely, if we serve while complaining, then they will learn to serve while complaining. Someone once said, "More is caught than taught." This is so true. We can teach our children all day long, but ultimately they will learn from our example. As we give them the example of cheerful service, we are expressing fondness to them and for them. If what they are "catching" from us is a complaining attitude, unthankful heart, and a sour disposition, then we need to change. And we can change…with our Savior's help.

Many times the issues we see and dislike in our children mirror our own issues. For example, have you ever heard something you did not like come out of your child's mouth only to realize that was exactly what you said earlier in the day? Take time to sit before the Lord and ask Him to reveal any wrong attitudes your children may be picking up on from your example. Or simply just watch your children and take note of the attitudes you see there and ask God if these are stemming from your own attitudes. And then repent of these things and ask God to train you in His ways— instead of following these old patterns of behavior. Ask Him specifically to replace these displeasing things with His ways. He can and will do it! Remain diligent in seeking God for this change. Most often it will be a process of daily renewal and will take time. But your diligence in seeking and asking will pay off!

Another way to practically show fondness for our children is to simply tell them we like them. It sounds simple, but as we verbally express our fondness for them, we show them they are valued. We instill the value God places on them through verbal affirmation. In the last few years, I have started simply telling my kids how special they are to me. I tell them they are my sweet girls or strong boys. I make a point to tell them how much we love them and how much God loves them. I am showing my fondness for them through my words to them. We as parents want our children to grow up being defined by how God views them rather than how the world views them. The desire is to express how much we value them and how much God values them. That our children truly are a blessing to us.

I have a friend who told me that her father used to daily take the time to tell her that he was happy she lived with them. That it brought him pleasure to be with her on a daily basis. When asked how this affected her, she responded that it caused her to feel highly valued. This high value placed upon her in turn caused her not to seek affection in any area other than God and her parents. Take time to tell your children you are fond of them. Make them feel valued through your words. Tell them they are special. Speak life to them, and it will impact them throughout their lives. If you haven't been doing this, don't beat yourself up about it. Just begin today…now even. Put down this book and go find your children and tell them how valuable they are to you and to God. Begin a new page in your relationship with your children. Begin to build them up instead of tearing them down. It will have eternal results! Proverbs tells us that a wise woman builds up her home, but a foolish woman tears it down with her hands…or her words.

What about tenderness? Colossians 3:12 tells us, "Therefore, as the elect of God, holy and beloved, put on tender mercies, kindness, humility, meekness, longsuffering." The opposite of tenderness is harshness. Tenderness is practically shown in our tone of voice and manner to our children. Do they feel comfortable coming and sharing a problem or issue with you knowing you won't come unglued? Do they expect compassion and tenderness when they approach you? Would you approach God if you expected harshness without compassion? No, we would be fearful to come to God if this were the case.

But God is tender and gentle with us. He shows us compassion and mercy, which we do not deserve. Once again, God and His relationship with us is our pattern for parenting. If God is tender and compassionate with His children, should we not be with ours? Of course we should. The first step is determining if we are showing tenderness or not. Take time to note your response to your children. Ask God to show you. You may even ask your children. But be ready for the answer! Then we take this information to the Lord in prayer and ask for forgiveness if needed. True repentance from sin means that we turn away from it. Ask God to train you in tenderness. Ask for specific opportunities to show tenderness instead of harshness. He will provide them. It may be slow going at first, but don't lose heart!

A practical contrast showing the difference between tenderness and harshness is when a child gets hurt. Tenderness says, "Are you all right, dear? Let me kiss it. You are fine now...go and play." Harshness says, "Suck it up. I don't want to hear it. Stop that crying." Harshness has no time for her children's problems or issues. Tenderness always makes time. Harshness repels, while tenderness draws near. Tenderness opens our children's hearts to us, while harshness closes their hearts. Does it take more time and effort to exhibit tenderness rather than harshness? Yes, it does. But it is a worthy investment made into our children. The Christian woman desires to do all things God's way and not her own. She will make the effort to determine what His ways are and then take time and effort to employ them as God leads.

What if we don't know what this tenderness looks like? What if our own mothers were not tender with us, but harsh? What if we did not have a mother around to show us that tenderness? If we have not experienced this tenderness in our own relationships, we can still demonstrate it to our children. This only comes as we draw near to God and ask Him to teach it to us. It is that simple. God's will for us is to live a holy life full of the characteristics we have been discussing. 1 Thessalonians 5:23–24 tells us, "Now may the God of peace Himself sanctify you completely; and may your whole spirit, soul, and body be preserved blameless at the coming of our Lord Jesus Christ. He who calls you is faithful, who also will do it." He who has called us is faithful and will sanctify us—clean us up, set us apart for God's work, and make us blameless. Ask for tenderness and take God at His Word! He will teach you and bring it to pass.

How can we take pleasure in our children? We take pleasure

in our children as we recognize God's hand in their creation. God has fearfully and wonderfully made them in His image. Just as we were marvelously designed, so were our children. Everything was placed just as God desired it. We and our children are the creation, while God is the Creator. The Creator takes pleasure in His creation. Just as an artist takes pleasure in his finished piece of art, so God finds pleasure in the creation of you and me. That is a remarkable thought. God is our Father, and as stated earlier, the pattern for parenting is found in our relationship with our Father in heaven. So as God takes pleasure in us, so we should also take pleasure in our children. But how do we that?

First, we can contemplate their frames. We can really ponder the design that went into their creation. We may look at their little hands and feet or hear their small voices and draw pleasure from that alone. When each of my and Owen's children was born, there was something different that brought me wonder and pleasure. I recall that with the first, it was just everything about him. With the next it was the tiny hands and feet, the third the sweet and kissable lips, and the last the perfectly formed ears. We can take pleasure in God's design of our children. If we don't find pleasure in God's creation of our children, we may ask Him to put that within us. Once again we come back to Matthew 7:7, if we ask in accordance with His will, we will receive.

Another way we can take pleasure in our children is to play with them. We can take time out of the day to sit down and play puppies, or a game, dance with them, or just to talk with them. We lose out on enjoying our kids sometimes because we are just too busy to enjoy them. I heard a couple say recently that they were "building a future" for their children now and that is why they never spend time with them. The response given in reply to that statement was that now is the time to be with your kids. What will it matter in fifteen years if you have a nest egg built for them but no relationship with them? Take the time to enjoy the children God has given into your care. Do it today. If you feel you have no time to do this, then ask the Lord to provide the time for you. Or move things around in your schedule. There may be things that really aren't as important as your children that are taking your time. Be willing to cut those things out for the more important opportunities—time with your children. Enjoy your children by taking the time to do so.

As you take the time to instill value through words, contemplate your children, and enjoy them, you will be pouring into them, or investing in their lives. Think of it like a bank account. Every moment you take to contemplate, talk to, play with, or enjoy your children is like a deposit into that account. The account will accrue "interest" over time. At the end of ten years, you will have a nice "nest egg" of love and relationship built within your children.

If your children are older or even adults, don't think that you can't begin doing this now. Start where you are and get on track with investing in your child or children. It is never too late to begin. The investment you make today in your children and endeavoring to enjoy them will pay off in the long run. Keep a long-term view of the time you put in today. Just as we keep our eyes fixed on the prize of Jesus Christ in this life, so we must also keep our eyes fixed on the prize of our long-term relationship with our children. And once again, if you do not presently enjoy your children, ask God to change your heart. He will.

Please have the understanding that you will not always enjoy your children. There will be times of discipline, bad attitudes, and crying. We are talking about an overall attitude of enjoying our children and not a moment-by-moment enjoyment. That would only occur if both you and your children were perfect. And we know that only One was perfect, Jesus the Christ.

We have seen how we instill the value God places through verbal affirmation, how we can have fondness for our children, tenderness in our dealings with them, and how we may develop an attitude of enjoying them. God has already equipped us to live these things out—now we must ask Him to bring us into them on a daily basis. He who has called us is faithful! 2 Peter 1:3 tells us that God has equipped us for everything pertaining to life and godliness. He alone can teach us and train us up in these areas. Don't think it impossible, dear ladies! With God, all things are possible!

LESSON 4 STUDY QUESTIONS

Training Up Our Children

A Christian woman trains her children up for God. She teaches and trains her children in the ways of her Lord. Proverbs 22:6 says, "Train up a child in the way he should go, And when he is old he will not depart from it." The woman following Christ puts in much time and energy on the home front. She spends many of her daily hours in training her children and directing them in the way they should go. This is all done for God's glory. Colossians 3:17 tells us to "do all in the name of the Lord Jesus." Let's look at what the Word tells us about training our children and how to practically do this on a daily basis.

1.   What do you think it means to train your children?

2.   Look up the following verses and write them out. Make a note of what each verse says about child training.

   a) Deuteronomy 6:4–7

   b) Proverbs 22:15

   c) Proverbs 13:24

   d) Colossians 3:21

3.   How can we apply the above verses in training our children up for God?

Our children are our disciples. Who else do we have the opportunity to teach on a daily basis? Let us not grow weary in training, for the reward is great! Even though we may not see immediate results, they will come in time. Remember that child training is here a little, there a little…precept upon precept and line upon line (Isaiah 26:11). We don't *have* to train them…we *get* to! It is our privilege to train up our children for our Lord.

Study Notes

CHAPTER 5

CHRISTIAN FRIENDSHIP

A woman in love with Jesus is a good friend to others. Jesus is the best Friend we have, and she is being conformed into His image. We are still sinners in need of our Savior and will fail in friendship from time to time. But overall, a disciple of Christ will have friendships based on the firm foundation of Jesus. Jesus should be at the center of our closest friendships. He should be the governing force behind each woman we let into our inner sphere of influence. What is the purpose of Christian friendship? The purpose is to help encourage growth in one another in our relationship with Christ. We are to mutually encourage each other as believers to seek God.

Friendships come in many shapes, forms, and packages. Our friends may be like us or completely the opposite of us. They may be single with no children, while we are married with children. They may have a career outside the home, while we are homemakers. They may be of different nationalities with different interests. There may be many differences between friends, but the unifying factor is Jesus. Have you ever met someone and felt a connection, only to find out she was a believer in the Lord Jesus? There is a sweet unity among true believers who are seeking God's purpose in their lives. Without this underlying unifying factor, we are at a disadvantage right off the bat.

A believer and a nonbeliever can only have a certain amount of intimacy. The nonbeliever will not be able to comprehend the relationship we have with our Lord and are therefore unable to understand the motivation of our hearts. They are not born again spiritually and have not received a new nature. Their eyes are still blinded from the truth. This is not to say we should not be friendly toward them. Quite the contrary! We are to be friendly to and love on nonbelievers. Our desire is the same as our Lord's—to see them receive eternal life. But we also know that we are not to be unequally yoked with a nonbeliever, even in a friendship. In other words, we should not associate on an intimate level with a non-Christian. And this means placing limitations on the relationships we have with them. We must seek our Lord in regard to what He desires in these areas.

When it comes to friendships, we must be careful who we allow into our lives and hearts. Over and over in Proverbs we are told not to keep company with those who are angry, dishonest, or evil. The purpose in this warning is found in Proverbs 22:24–25, "Make no friendship with an angry man, And with a furious man do not go, Lest you learn his ways And set a snare for your soul."

If we keep company or allow a friendship with a person in this state, then she will rub off on us! We will set a snare for our own soul! Have you been around a person who is constantly complaining and then find yourself doing it as well? She has rubbed off on you, and you may fall into that sin. Proverbs 13:20 tells us, "He who walks with wise men will be wise, But the companion of fools will be destroyed."

We must ask the Lord for His guidance with friendships. He will bring the perfect friend at the perfect time. The Lord has at times removed friendships from me by having the ladies move away. I realized that sometimes friendships were just for a season and were a gift from God. These friends moved on in accordance with God's will. Although sad, I realized that it was for my benefit, because I needed that time to refocus on my relationship with my Lord. God has allowed me to fellowship with some of the most wonderful women! I met them at the Lord's direction and in His timing. They have proved to be amazing ladies in love with Jesus. Just the friends I would have picked if I could have picked them. A true gift from God.

These friendships are all different. Some of these women are in situations similar to mine, while others are miles apart. Despite our differences, God has united us together in Him. I am blessed to have these women to speak into my life and heart. They are a gift, and I know I am a gift to them as well because they have told me as much. God gives good gifts to His children, sometimes in the form of people He places in our lives.

I am still learning how to be a good friend to these sweet ladies. In the beginning of my Christian walk, I understood that God desired me to be a good friend, but I didn't know how to do that. My relationships to that point had been superficial, partially because of my inability to be that good friend to someone else. Once I came to Christ, I desired Christian friendship and a mature Christian lady to mentor me but had trouble finding either of these. I never did obtain a mentor, and it was years before God began to bring solid and healthy friendships into my life.

Looking back, I see now that God had a plan. He was training me in this time to seek Him first and not look to a person. He desired that I learn from Him alone and not from a mentor. Mentors are wonderfully helpful, but in my case, God knew what was best for me and so did not allow one. He probably had an idea I would place a mentor on the pedestal of my heart, and He wanted to be on that pedestal! And so I learned to ask God to teach me and to go directly to Him with my problems and issues. He taught me much on being a good Christian friend over the years. We will begin by looking at what makes a good friend in someone and then move from there to how we can be that friend to others.

What makes a good friend? As I prayed about this, these things came to mind. The first is a listening ear. A good friend listens. She cares about what you are saying and takes the time to really listen to you. She is listening not only for what you are saying, but also for what you are not saying. She asks questions to draw out your inner self and true feelings in a matter. She studies how to answer after listening. Proverbs 15:28 says, "The heart of the righteous studies how to answer." Proverbs 17:27 says, "He who has knowledge spares his words." This friend will study your demeanor to determine if you really are doing well when you say you are. She will take the time and expend the energy to really be there for you and to hear what you are saying.

Quite a few years back, God convicted me on listening. I was thinking of what I would answer back instead of really listening to my friend. I needed to stop thinking of what I was going to say in response. I needed to learn to really hear what a friend, or anyone, was saying. God had to train me to truly listen. A good friend will offer a listening ear.

The second is that a good friend will be trustworthy. She will not share her friends' faults with another. This friend will not broadcast another's struggles abroad. There will be no rumor floating about regarding what you just shared. This friend is a woman of honor and integrity. She is the kind whom you do not have to tell not to say anything. Proverbs 11:13 tells us that "A talebearer reveals secrets, But he who is of a faithful spirit conceals a matter." A trustworthy friend has this faithful spirit. Proverbs 17:9 says, "He who covers a transgression seeks love, But he who repeats a matter separates friends." A good friend will keep a confidence where it belongs, in her heart. She is worthy of your trust.

The third thing that makes a good friend is that she is encouraging. She will build her friend up in words and actions. She waits on God for His timing and words for her friend. The encouraging friend never tears her friend down. She will never deliberately say something to make her friend feel badly. Instead she will look for ways and opportunities as God provides them to build her friend up. "Pleasant words are like a honeycomb, Sweetness to the soul and health to the bones" (Proverbs 16:24). This friend brings sweetness to the soul and health to the bones of her companions. "Anxiety in the heart of man causes depression, But a good word makes it glad" (Proverbs 12:25). She uses words of encouragement to make her friend's heart glad. The encouraging friend sees when her friend is feeling low and brings that good word at just the right time. She uses her words and actions to help point her friend to God. She builds up her friend in spirit. A good friend encourages.

And the last thing on this short list is mercy. A good friend is merciful. This friend will overlook and forgive offenses. She will show mercy when you sin. She will not hold a grudge over a mistake you made. She will forgive and forget. This friend will also demonstrate mercy to your family. She will love in spite of character flaws and pray with you for growth in these areas. Proverbs 17:17 says, "A friend loves at all times." A good friend does not only love when things are smooth but also when they are rough. She does not take off at the first sign of strife or struggle. This friend sticks with you. She shows mercy when offended and loves at all times. She shows that love does cover a multitude of sins. A good friend is merciful.

We have seen some things that make a good friend. These are things we may put on our friend shopping list. Now let's look at how we can be that good friend to others. To be a good friend to others, we must first be in a right relationship with God. The number one requirement of being a good Christian friend to others is that we seek God first and foremost in our lives. This may seem like a strange thing in reference to friendship, but it is vital for a healthy relationship. Ultimately, everything comes back to our relationship with our Lord. If our relationship with God is right, then our other relationships will be right, as much as it depends on us, that is. We cannot control another person's behavior, only our own. Being a good friend to others will come naturally over time as we consistently put God first in our lives. Matthew 6:33 states, "Seek ye first the kingdom of God and His righteousness, and all these things will be added unto you." Our first focus in friendship is Jesus the Christ. From there we can take the list compiled above and apply it to ourselves.

We must have that listening ear. We must take the time to truly listen to what our friends are saying. We need to ask God to teach us to listen. It seems difficult to listen sometimes. It is difficult to be still for a time and truly listen to another person.

Instead of thinking of what we will say next, we should be listening to the other person's words. God will teach us if we ask Him to. We need to talk less and listen more. We need to ask those questions that will draw our friends out of themselves. We need to practice not talking. That sounds strange, but if we really want to hear someone, then we need to practice self-control in our speech. We just need to shut our mouths for a while and let someone else talk. And then really hear them. Really hear where they are, what struggles they have, where they are at with the Lord, and how we can be in prayer for them. We need to have a listening ear.

We ourselves must be worthy of the trust of others. We must never share our friends' struggles or inner thoughts with others unless we have their express permission to do so. Gossip is a good way to end a friendship. It divides friends quickly and effectively. And it can hurt deeply. A Christian woman should not ever engage in gossip. We are warned many times in Scripture to control the tongue. This is for good reason. James 3 tells us that "the tongue is a fire, a world of iniquity." James likens the tongue to kindling a forest fire. The tongue is a flame that can potentially cause a forest fire. Gossip or slander spreads like fire. As James says later in the chapter, "these things ought not to be so." Ladies, let us be women who do not partake of this sin in any form. Be the friend you desire to have...one who is trustworthy.

Encouragement is key in a friendship. We must build a friend up and never tear her down. We need to edify, or uplift, one another in the faith. We must strengthen one another and lift each other up. If sin or something concerning her walk with the Lord needs to be brought up, it must be done in love and in an encouraging fashion. This means we need to wait on the Lord for His words.

We have a saying at our house: "We only speak encouraging and uplifting words." If the words coming out of your mouth are discouraging, then stop speaking. If your tone of voice is wrong, then stop speaking. If your attitude is wrong, then stop speaking. Take a moment with the Lord and get right with Him and then begin the conversation again with God at the helm. We as ladies representing Jesus must speak words of life and truth to our friends. Proverbs 12:18 says that "the tongue of the wise promotes health." We must bring spiritual health and wellness to our friends as we encourage them.

And lastly, we ourselves must be merciful. We must show mercy and grace to our friends. We must overlook and forgive their trespasses. When offenses come, we must forgive and move on. James 3:2 tells us that "we all stumble in many things." The word for stumble can mean to sin or offend. We all stumble, sin, or offend in many things. This is the reality of life and friendship. We must show mercy and overlook these offenses, knowing that we also offend, stumble, and sin in many things. As God's grace is shown to us, we must in return show this grace to others. 1 Timothy 1:14 says that "the grace of our Lord was exceedingly abundant." The word used for exceedingly abundant means to superabound. God's grace superabounds to us.

The Lord gave me a picture of this superabounding grace some time ago. We have cherry trees. I had been pondering this verse and asking God to really bring it home to me. Early one morning I was picking cherries. We had an incredible crop. There was no way I could reach them all due to my ladder height. I looked up, and it dawned on me. This tree was superabounding in cherries. There were so many that I could not get them all. That is how God's grace is. There is so much that we can't get it all. So much that we must share it with others. It must superabound to our friends through us as we experience it. The Lord's grace never stops flowing. Neither must ours. To be a good friend, we must be merciful and show God's grace.

We have seen that the purpose of Christian friendship is to encourage a mutual growth in our relationships with Jesus Christ. Christian friendship should not be a hindrance but a help to the maintenance of a life in continual fellowship with God. We have seen that Christian friendship must be based on our mutual love for Jesus Christ. We looked at what we would desire in a friend from a listening ear to being merciful. And then we applied that same list to ourselves as a protocol for us being that good friend to another. This list is by far not exhaustive but is just a small portion of important things.

Finally, let us look at the benefit of Christian friendship to us.

Why go to the trouble of building and maintaining a friendship with another believer? Ecclesiastes 4:9–12 says, "Two are better than one, Because they have a good reward for their labor. For if they fall, one will lift up his companion. But woe to him who is alone when he falls, For he has no one to help him up. Again, if two lie down together, they will keep warm; But how can one be warm alone? Though one may be overpowered by another, two can withstand him." These verses tell us that two are better than one for a few reasons. One is that they will have a good reward for their labor. Two can get more done than one. A friend can offer assistance in labor. There are many jobs that just seem easier if a friend is there to help. And she also may be able to bring to the table gifts or experiences we do not have, which yields a better reward from the labor.

The second reason is that if one friend falls, the other will lift him or her up. When a friend is down and reaches out to us, we can lift her up and point her back in the direction of our Lord. And when we are down, a friend will do the same for us. This is encouragement at its finest. These verses tell us that it is detrimental if a woman falls alone, because she will have no friend to lift her up. A friend can encourage and comfort when needed and receives the same encouragement and comfort when she's in need.

Lastly, one may be overpowered by an enemy, but two can withstand. When the enemy of our souls comes and buffets, or surrounds, us, our friends can stand with us in prayer against this attack. Friends can go on the offensive with us. Christian friends can give good counsel based upon the Word of God. They can support us by supplying us with Scripture as we need it. They can help us to withstand the attack or endure the trial.

Last year, my mother was in the hospital for two weeks. It was serious, and we honestly didn't know if she would leave that hospital. Some dear friends stepped up in my time of need and took turns watching my children so that I might be able to go and be with her during this time. This service was invaluable to me. Along with this, they were supporting me in prayer and providing encouragement for me along the way. I know that these dear ladies are here for me if I need them. And conversely, they know that I am there for them if they need me. One may be overpowered, but two can withstand!

And so we see that Christian friends are valuable to us in our walk through life. They are a gift from God. It is good to maintain those relationships based upon Christ and to ask God to teach us to be the friend He desires us to be. If you feel unequipped to be this type of friend, just ask God to show you. Be the friend that you would want. Keep your focus on Him alone, and as Matthew tells us, "All these things shall be added unto you." If God is in the process of teaching me, He will most certainly teach you as well.

LESSON 5 STUDY QUESTIONS

Christian Friendships

A Christian woman should be a good friend. What does being a good friend look like anymore? We are living in an era unequaled for broken relationships. Society tells us it is all about "me." There are few healthy relationships to look to for an example. But we still have the Word of God, which remains our source of truth through the ages. There is still hope amid all of the confusion to find out what a good friend looks like and how we can be that good friend to others! Let's find out what our Guidebook tells us about friendship.

1.   What characteristics would you look for in a friend if you were "friend shopping"?

2.   Look up the following verses and write them out. Make a note of what each verse says about friendship.

a) Proverbs 17:17

b) Proverbs 18:24

c) Proverbs 27:17

3.   How can we be a good friend to others?

4.   What is the purpose of Christian friendships? Why would we take the time to build these relationships with others?

5.   It has been said that healthy friendships in a believer's life are indicators of a healthy relationship with the Lord. Do you agree or disagree with this statement? Why?

_____

_____

_____

_____

_____

_____

_____

_____

_____

_____

_____

_____

_____

_____

_____

_____

Study Notes

Study Notes

CHAPTER 6

A Christian woman should be gracious when offenses arise. This means that she is full of unmerited favor toward the offending party. The follower of Jesus extends mercy and forgiveness to those who have offended. She is not easily offended and is quick to forgive. This can be incredibly difficult to practically carry out because of how our flesh—our human nature with its frailties and passions—wants to respond. The flesh reacts to an offense with the desire to lash out, to withhold forgiveness, and to become bitter. But Jesus requires something different of us when offenses arise. He requires mercy, love, forgiveness, and grace. In order to apply these traits the way Jesus requires, we must sacrifice our flesh. We must lay our fleshly desires of anger, bitterness, and revenge upon the altar and allow Jesus to pour His forgiveness and love through us.

This sacrifice may not be just a onetime event. We may need to sacrifice the flesh over and over in regard to the offense and offender. The Christian walk is a thousand deaths to self. But we must remember that a death to self means more room for Christ. Let's look at the different types of offenses, examples of them, and how to deal with them. Please keep in mind that this is a difficult area for us due to our self-preservation and self-right. Keep a teachable spirit in this, and God will show you much. We will start by looking at what offense is.

The words offense, offend, offenses, and offended are used often in Scripture. I compiled over two pages of references to these words from the Bible. Why is it so frequently used? Could it be that we will offend others a lot? And that others will offend us a lot? We are told in Scripture that we will offend in many things. Logically, if we are offending often, then someone else will be offending us often. The word for offense as found in Scripture carries the meaning of enticing to sin, stumbling, tripping up, to err, or fail. The definition of offense is the act of offending by any sin, wrong, or fault. Also that which injures the feelings, causes displeasure, or provokes. The definition of offend means to give displeasure or affront. Along with this, it also carries the meaning of causing one to sin or stumble.

There are two basic types of offenses. The first is being a stumbling block. Either someone else is a stumbling block of offense to you, or you are to them. We see an example of Jesus choosing not to be a stumbling block of offense in Matthew 17:24–27. In this section we see the temple tax collector coming to Peter and asking if Jesus pays the temple tax. Peter replied that He did.

Jesus conversed with Peter and let him know that He was not bound to pay the temple tax but would do so anyway so as not to offend the tax collectors. "Nevertheless, lest we offend them, go to the sea, cast in a hook, and take the fish that comes up first. And when you have opened its mouth, you will find a piece of money; take that and give it to them for Me and you" (Matthew 17:27).

Jesus didn't need to pay the temple tax. According to Malachi 3:1, the temple belonged to Him! But in order not to offend the temple tax collector, Jesus told Peter to get the coin to pay the tax as he was directed above "lest we offend them." The Greek word used here for offend means to entice to sin, stumble, entrap, or trip up. Jesus knew that His actions or lack thereof could potentially cause offense. There are always reactions to our actions. If Jesus would not have paid the tax, the tax collector could have reacted in sin—he would have been enticed to sin. The tax man didn't know that Jesus owned the temple. He didn't understand that Jesus was not bound by our earthly rules. In this instance, Jesus chose to pay the tax that He did not have to in order to avoid offending or enticing this man to sin. Jesus chose not to offend.

We as Christ-following women have a choice in this matter of offense as well. We may entice others to sin. Or we may choose not to entice others to sin. Our actions will cause reactions. We may not always see the immediate effects of our actions, but there will be reactions in some form. People around us may not know that we have liberty in Christ. They don't understand that we have a heavenly citizenship and are simply pilgrims passing through.

There will be times when in order not to offend or entice others to sin that we do not act upon our liberties. Jesus is our example in this. He had the liberty not to pay the temple tax, but He paid it anyway. Jesus humbled Himself and took action not to offend. There are times when we also must take action, or not take action, in order not to offend. Let me give you a practical example of this

My husband, Owen, and I were invited to a dinner party with a mix of believers and unbelievers. There were a few other Christian couples at our table. The other couples at the table with us began ordering and drinking alcohol. Owen and I did not partake. Could it be possible that the Christians who were drinking placed a stumbling block in the way of the nonbelievers in coming to know Christ? Is it possible that the group who was drinking could entice the other believers to sin? We don't always know the backgrounds of others. There may be a struggle with alcohol in the past. There is a possibility of ensnaring them back into drinking through seeing others doing it. Did these folks have a right to drink? Yes, we have liberty to have a glass of wine (but not to get drunk). But in this case, they should have laid down their liberty to do this for the sake of the others around them.

Owen and I have come to a personal conclusion from Scripture that it is safer for Christians not to drink in public. It is better to keep it in the privacy of your own home if you choose to do this. This way there is no possibility of causing another believer to stumble or showing a confusing witness for Christ to a nonbeliever. May we not give anyone a reason to sin or a cause to stumble. Even believers can be caught in the trap of drinking in excess if they see others doing it. They may be weak in the faith and get drawn in. We would be horrified to learn that we had ever caused someone to stumble in this way!

Paul says in Romans 14:21, "It is good neither to eat meat nor drink wine nor do anything by which your brother stumbles or is offended or is made weak." This principle of nonoffense and laying down our liberties for the sake of others can be applied in many areas of life. Jesus gave up His right to not pay the temple tax to avoid offending someone and enticing him to sin. May we also be willing to give up our rights in order not to offend. May we view these things in light of eternity! Laying down our rights in an area in order not to trip up a brother or sister in Christ may reap eternal rewards. On the other side of the coin, our lack of laying down our rights may result in eternal consequence. We just don't know the outcome of things or how our actions may or may not affect someone else.

The second type of offense is offending by personal sin. James 3:2 tells us, "For we all offend in many things." The word for offend here is to sin, fail, err, or trip up. We all sin. We all fail. If we are around others in any capacity, then our sins or failings will affect others. Our actions will cause reactions. Proverbs 18:19 says,

"A brother offended is harder to win than a strong city." The word offended in this verse means to turn away because of a trespass. When our sin affects someone else, it causes a breach in the relationship. It's like we are traveling down the same road with a person—then we sin, and our paths diverge. We fall out of fellowship with her. The same principle applies in our relationship to the Lord. When we sin, we diverge from our fellowship with God. We become out of alignment with God's heart and out of fellowship with Him.

What causes this breach in our fellowship with others? The breach is caused by sin in any form. It could be an unkind word, a thoughtless action, pride, gossip, or any number of other things. Just as sin will take us out of fellowship with God, so sin will take us out of fellowship with others. That is until we make it right and allow God's love and forgiveness to flow.

A friend of mine gave me an example of this. My friend Sophie had a breach in her relationship with her siblings for many years because of an offense due to personal sin. A close family member had died, and some things were said by one sibling that offended the others. And then some things were said back that in turn offended the first sibling. Personal sin came out in a time of intense stress and grief. The words of this one family member enticed the others to sin, which they did. An action of sin caused a reaction of sin.

These brothers and sisters ended up being out of fellowship

for almost ten years! The initial action of personal sin that was portrayed through offensive comments caused anger in Sophie. Anger is a response to hurt. And with anger comes the desire to lash out, which she did. Sophie was offended or enticed to sin by her sibling. Hurt was abounding in this family, and it came out in the unproductive response of personal sin toward one another.

The beginning of resolving this issue came with small kindnesses. Sophie's sister began reaching out in small ways and showing kindness. But Sophie wasn't ready to forgive until her relationship with Jesus was right. She had a distant relationship with the Lord, and He had to do an incredible work in her heart so that she could forgive and receive forgiveness. As of today, these siblings have a wonderful relationship with one another. All has been forgiven, and the story is used for God's glory. Sophie's advice is this, "Do not be easily offended, and be quick to forgive. Do not let the enemy rob you of fellowship with your loved ones." In this account we see how a family fell out of fellowship with one another due to personal sin. But we also see God's plan for restoration in those situations. We see how an action caused a reaction. God desires something better for us in our reactions to offenses. He desires us not to be easily offended but to be quick to forgive. In other words, God desires us to be gracious in offenses.

We have looked at what offense is and the two basic types of it. We have seen some examples of what offense can look like and the outcome of it. If you have realized that you have been inadvertently offending someone by your actions, then stop behaving that way. Ask the Lord if He desires you to apologize for this, and go in God's timing to do so. If you are out of fellowship with a loved one, a friend, or anyone due to your own personal sin…bring it before the Lord this moment! Ask Him to forgive you. And then go make it right with the offended party. As Sophie advised, may we not allow the enemy to rob us of precious time with our loved ones. Take action in this situation today! In the next chapter we will look at what the reality of a Christian woman being practically gracious in offense looks like.

LESSON 6 STUDY QUESTIONS

Graciousness in Offenses

A Christian woman should be gracious when offenses arise. This means she is full of unmerited favor toward the offending party. The Christian woman extends mercy and forgiveness. This can be difficult. The flesh tells us to lash out, not to forgive, and certainly not to love. But Jesus requires something different of us. He requires mercy, love, and forgiveness. His requirement is a sacrifice of the flesh, a death to our "self." But a death to self always means more room for Christ! Let's look at what the Bible tells us about offenses and how to deal with them.

1.   What kind of offenses have you dealt with? How did you react to them?

2.   Look up the following verses. Record what stands out to you in each one.

   a) Luke 1:1–4

   b) Proverbs 17:9

   c) Proverbs 17:14

   d) Matthew 6:14–15

3.   What does the Bible tell us we should do if we become offended?

4.   Can a friendship continue after one party is offended? What must be done for it to continue?

5.   How can we move on from an offense? How can we begin the healing process after we received an injustice or we doled out the injustice?

_____

_____

_____

_____

_____

_____

_____

_____

_____

_____

_____

_____

_____

_____

_____

_____

Study Notes

Study Notes

CHAPTER 7

I n the last chapter we answered the question of what offense is—enticing someone to sin or causing her to stumble. We saw what it looks like and some examples of it. Now we will ponder the question of what it actually means to be gracious in offense. What does this look like on a practical level? When you are offended, how can you practically show graciousness? Back in chapter one, we learned that in order to show love to others, we must first experience Christ's love. The same principle applies with grace. In order to show God's grace to another, we must first experience that grace ourselves. It would be difficult to teach someone to ride a unicycle if you yourself had never mastered it. There is a credibility we receive when God teaches us something and allows us to teach it to others and causes it to be well received. A few years ago after being asked to speak at a ladies' event, I was praying about teaching on a certain subject. While in prayer on it, God made it clear I should not teach on that theme. When asking why, I received the answer that I had not learned that topic on a heart level yet. I only knew it on an intellectual level and would be unable to offer a practical example.

Presenting the Word is never wrong...but God has consistently wanted me to share with others only what I have learned at His feet and actually put into practice. So if you have not experienced God's grace on a heart level, ask Him to teach it to you. If you have not learned how to be gracious when offense comes, ask God to train you in this. As we saw in prior chapters, when we ask in accordance with God's will, He will answer us. God desires to give us good gifts, and if His grace isn't a good gift, then I don't know what is!

Learning to be gracious when offended is a process. It takes time. In my experience it is trial and error. God awakens the desire to be gracious when offense arises. Then we ask for it, and He begins a work of grace in our hearts by teaching us. And then we begin stepping out in obedience to God's teaching. We actually have to do it! James 1:22 says, "But be doers of the word and not hearers only, deceiving yourselves." We deceive ourselves if we hear but do not do. This is where the rubber meets the road. This is the trial-and-error portion. Maybe it is best if we call it the obedience-and-error portion. We step out in obedience but know that we will fail as we learn.

When a child is learning a new skill, such as how to walk, she doesn't get it all at once. She tries and tries again, falling down each time. But then she gets up again and tries once more. We will fail. But God is gracious. We shall just get up again and try once more.

We are not determined by the fall but by the rise after the fall. Eventually that little child will walk. This does not mean that she will not ever stumble or fall down again, for that will happen. Even as adults we trip occasionally. But we have learned a skill that will serve us for a lifetime. The training process for learning to be gracious in offense is a difficult one, but it is well worth the difficulty. And it will serve us for a lifetime, because we know that offense will come for the remainder of our time here on Earth.

Do you have anyone in your life who consistently offends? I think we all have at least one person, if not more. These can be difficult relationships. Maybe the person is a coworker, a family member, a friend, a fellow volunteer, or someone in your church family. The purpose of these folks is to grow us in our relationship to the Lord. We are like a piece of wood, and they are like the sandpaper. They rub us against our "grain." It can be uncomfortable. But we also know that the sandpaper takes all the rough edges off the piece of wood. The wood becomes smooth and useful for a project. The wood that could not have been used before, now has the potential for use. The offensive person works in this way as well. As we are in relationships with these difficult folks, our rough edges are sanded away. This happens when offense comes and we take it to the Lord and allow Him to teach us through it. Through this process, we become smoother and more useful to Him. This only occurs if we are surrendered to God's will. We must be teachable to be taught.

God has been teaching me much in this area. A few years ago, Owen and I realized that we were not loving others to the extent that we felt Christ was asking. We asked Him to teach us to love as He would have us love. After praying this, God brought us into difficult situations where our love just wouldn't cut it, and we had to begin to learn how to allow Him to love through us. Offenses abounded, and we learned that God desires a gracious and loving response to these. This is completely opposite from what the natural man within us desires to do.

Recently some comments were made to me that I really didn't know what to do with. They were unloving, and I could have easily taken offense to them. The Lord allowed me a collected and gentle response. Afterward, anger flamed up, and I realized that the comment had hurt me. The temptation to sin had arisen.

We need to differentiate between temptation and sin. Temptation is the initial thought or feeling as it pops into our heads or rises up. Sin is one option of what we choose to do with that thought or feeling. Will we sin, or will we reject this thought or feeling? I had a choice at this point. I could continue in anger and let bitterness seep in, or I could do it God's way. We are going to examine both of these options. First, let's look at our way.

Our way is the way of the flesh. If we respond in our flesh, we will lash out, be filled with anger, become bitter toward the offender, and stay out of fellowship with her or him and with God. Sin separates us from true fellowship with God and others. When we react in our flesh, it is sin. We may say, "But they are the ones who offended us!" We try to justify our responses to their offensive words, actions, or attitudes. The idea here is that they have done the wrong, so we have a right to be upset with them.

When we went to the cross and laid down our burdens there, we also laid down our rights." 1 Corinthians 6:20 says, "For you were bought at a price; therefore glorify God in your body and in your spirit, which are God's." We belong to God. We have no right to react to sin with more sin. Remember the saying "two wrongs don't make a right"? We as Christian women are to glorify God in our bodies and spirits, knowing that we belong to God. This is a hard thing to receive—to understand and accept. But it is in the hardest things to receive and live out that a woman finds the most liberty in her relationship with Christ.

Can you imagine if we reacted in God's way and not our way? There would be such freedom in that. We would no longer be upset by what folks say, or carry it around with us. We burden ourselves with these offenses. But that is not God's desire for us. It is not His will for us to carry these things around. Matthew 11:28 tells us, "Come to Me, all you who labor and are heavy laden, and I will give you rest." The word in Greek for labor means to be fatigued from hard work and the toil of life. The word for heavy laden in Greek carries the meaning of overburdening ourselves with the issues of life, either our own or someone else's. To load ourselves up. Isn't that what we do when we are offended? We load ourselves up with what is more than likely someone else's issue and carry it around for a while. It is burdensome. It weighs us down, and it is difficult to carry, for we are not designed to carry it.

It is as if we each have a bucket. We carry this bucket around with us and put in our troubles, worries, burdens, and other people's offenses against us. Soon enough, we find our bucket is full. If we continue to carry this burden, we will be weary. We will feel heavy laden and burdened. We will be unhappy and complaining women. Bitterness will seep in and take root. The burden of offense we are carrying will consume us. This is the way of the flesh. But Jesus invites us to come to Him if we are weary or heavy laden, and He will give us rest. If your life bucket is full of yuck, simply come to Jesus and surrender all the contents to Him. Don't spend another minute carrying around a burden you were not meant to carry. Give Him the offense this very moment! He will give rest to the weary!

Now let's look at God's way of responding to offense. We know that God's way is the way of love, mercy, compassion, and longsuffering. In Exodus 34:6–7, God proclaimed the name of the Lord to Moses and said, "The LORD, the LORD God, merciful and gracious, longsuffering, and abounding in goodness and truth…" From this section we see that God is merciful, gracious, longsuffering, and abounding in goodness and truth. We know that Jesus is the exact image of God the Father. And we also know that Jesus is our example and that we are being conformed into His image. So we also should be merciful, gracious, longsuffering, and abounding in goodness and truth.

We are sinners in a fallen state and know that we will make mistakes, but our aim is Jesus. God's way in responding to offense is that we would exhibit these characteristics. God's way is that we would be merciful to offenders. That we would be gracious to them and demonstrate unmerited favor. That we would be longsuffering. Do they deserve it? Probably not. But then again, neither do we. When we offend someone, we definitely want forgiveness, mercy, and grace. Let's give those who offend us what we desire!

How does this happen practically? First, remember that this is not step one and then step two. It is a living relationship between us and Jesus. Ask Him to show you how to respond. With that being said, it is sometimes helpful to have practical examples based on Scripture to help us.

Let's return to the example of what was said to me. The comments were made. Through the grace of God, my response was gentle. Later, anger flamed as I thought about what was said. The first option, as we saw above, is the way of the flesh. The second option is God's way, the way of the Word. In following the way of the Word, I would immediately take my anger to the Lord. 1 Peter 5:6–7 tells us, "Therefore humble yourselves under the mighty hand of God, that He may exalt you in due time, casting all your care upon Him, for He cares for you." It requires humility to lay down what we perceive as our right to anger and ask God to show us His way in offenses. Jesus desires us to come to Him and cast all our cares upon Him. Casting our cares upon Jesus allows us to not carry that burden of offense. We may need to cast those cares and burdens upon the Lord more than once, maybe many times!

The next step in God's way of responding to offense is to forgive. First we bring the offense to Him, and then we forgive the offender. Colossians 3:12–13 says, "Therefore, as the elect of God, holy and beloved, put on tender mercies, kindness, humility, meekness, longsuffering; bearing with one another, and forgiving one another, if anyone has a complaint against another; even as Christ forgave you, so you also must do." We are to bear with one another and forgive one another when complaints arise. Matthew 6:14 tells us, "For if you forgive men their trespasses, your heavenly Father will also forgive you. But if you do not forgive men their trespasses, neither will your Father forgive your trespasses." We must forgive when offenses rise. Not only because God tells us to but for our own benefit. Unforgiveness can be an ugly thing.

As Christian women who love Jesus, we should be putting on the sweet things of the Lord. We should be allowing God to adorn us with His beautiful garments of submission, love, tenderness, and graciousness. When we refuse to forgive, it is like we are taking a dirty and torn garment and putting it on ourselves. The lovely garments God has provided and clothed us with cannot be seen underneath the nastiness of the cloak of unforgiveness. We cannot be further molded into the image of Christ until we remove this defiling garment. Let's cast the stained cloak off and resume being clothed with God's beauty! We do this by forgiving the person who offended us.

You may ask, "What if they have not asked to be forgiven?" In the example I gave above of the hurtful comments, the person never apologized. No more was ever said of it, and I did not feel compelled by God to bring it up. We as women want to talk things out and gain closure in situations. But the reality of it is, there will not always be closure in this way. God can bring a closing of the situation in our hearts when we come to Him with it, humble ourselves, and forgive the person involved.

After forgiveness comes the letting go. When God forgives us, the offense is never brought up again. Micah 7:19 says, "He will again have compassion on us, And will subdue our iniquities. You will cast all our sins into the depths of the sea." God casts our sins into the depths of the sea. There is no doubt that He does not go out "fishing" for them later to show us once again what we did. Regarding God's forgiveness of sins, Corrie ten Boom said in her book Tramp for the Lord, "They are now cast into the deepest sea and a sign is put up that says NO FISHING ALLOWED" (CLC Publications, 2011 ed.). We are forgiven, and the sins are not ever thrown back in our faces by God.

This principle was adopted by Owen and I in our marriage. Once an offense is forgiven between us, it is never brought up again. It is no longer remembered and totally forgiven. We can't tell you the last thing we were upset at each other about, because it is all gone. We keep short accounts with one another, getting right when necessary and not carrying things around. This is the letting go of the offense. We have a choice on whether we pick it up and carry it around with us in our arsenal to use at a later date or to just let it go. I have seen the arsenal format played out in marriages, and it is never a pretty sight. If we are consistently bringing up the past, we may need to examine our hearts to see if we have truly forgiven the offense. And then we need to let it go. It's like placing a toy boat in a stream flowing under a bridge. Once the boat floats under that bridge, we can't see it anymore. The same of the offense—we forgive and let it go and then should not see it anymore.

The comments made to me by a friend were forgiven although no further conversation was had in regard to it, no apology was made. And then it was let go like that little toy boat swept down the stream. It was gone and remembered no more. If it arises in my mind, I will bring it back to the Lord and surrender it to Him once again. And so we see that God's way in responding to offense is to bring the offense before Him and seek His counsel in the situation, forgive the offense, and let it go.

What about the aftermath? How do we respond to the offender after we have forgiven the fault? It all depends on the offense. Was it a rude comment? A careless word? A forgotten coffee date? Do these rude comments occur often? Are there many forgotten coffee dates? There may be a time and place to speak truth in love into the offender's heart. We have to seek God in this! Do not step into conversation with someone who has hurt you without first seeking your Father's counsel. Ask the Lord to show you if He wants you to bring it up. And if so, ask Him for the specific words to use and the right spirit to say them in. Never approach another in anger. If you are still angry, then wait. Never approach without God's leading. And don't do it until your heart is right in the matter.

Let's give a practical example of this. Let's say that Mary has offended you by making hurtful comments on an ongoing basis. She has not approached you asking for forgiveness and doesn't seem to see anything wrong with her behavior. You have brought the matter to the Lord each time as well as have been praying for her personally on a regular basis. After each offense, you have forgiven and moved on without a grudge. You have asked God if you should approach her and have not felt prompted to...until now. How do you do it? The Bible has all we need.

Matthew 18 has a guideline for us in this matter. Verses 15–17 tell us, "Moreover if your brother sins against you, go and tell him his fault between you and him alone. If he hears you, you have gained your brother. But if he will not hear, take with you one or two more, that 'by the mouth of two or three witnesses every word may be established.' And if he refuses to hear them, tell it to the church. But if he refuses even to hear the church, let him be to you like a heathen and a tax collector."

You would go to Mary by yourself and tell her your concerns. Of course, this has to be done in love. More than likely, Mary will not have realized she had been hurtful and will ask for forgiveness. But if she does not, you must seek the Lord and determine if He would have you move forward or let it go. In the case of feeling God leading to move forward, you would bring a trustworthy Christian along with you and reiterate your concerns. If Mary still rejects what you are saying, then you take it to the spiritual leadership of your fellowship, if she attends with you.

This is a big deal and a lengthy process, so we must make sure that we only do it at the Lord's leading and for something that it is worthy of. The offender must actually be sinning. It can't just be that we don't like something about that person or that her personality annoys us. We wouldn't take this step because the person has a personality we don't mesh with. We just need to get over that stuff and not be petty. We are talking about sin. We are talking about disobedience to God's Word. Make sure that the matter you are bringing before the offender is valid in light of the Bible. In the case of Mary and the mean things said, more than likely only the first portion will be used. An example of moving through the entire process in Matthew 18 may be sexual immorality, cheating, or any other number of things.

A friend of mine and Owen's recently did something we didn't approve of. Was it sin? Not specifically to us. But it was not respectful of us and our family. This particular thing has happened a few times. I brought it to the Lord each time and did not feel led to say anything to this friend before. But this time I did. And so I spent time in prayer about it and asked God for His words and timing. He provided both. It turned out to be a very short conversation at the end of a visit with no hard feelings afterward. And from there we just resumed the friendship with no more thought of the subject. We just brought the person back into the fellowship and love of our family. That was that.

But when offenses seriously injure you, your spouse, or your children, you may need to step away from the persons involved for a time so that they can prove themselves. Sometimes offenses requires us to step away permanently. Our first priority is the physical and spiritual safety of our families. Jesus tells us to be wise as serpents and harmless as doves.

We need to be wise in these situations. For example, if someone offends by stealing your computer, then you probably won't give the thief access to your home unattended in the future. That would be foolish. We are to be harmless as doves in that we are blameless before men, we forgive, we move on, and we love. But also we are to be wise as serpents. Seek God's counsel after a serious offense as to what He would have you do in regard to continuing or not continuing fellowship with the offender. You may also want to seek godly counsel from those around you whom you trust—your pastor, your Bible study teacher, or a solid friend.

Just keep in mind to relate the information to the trusted advisor in a manner pleasing to the Lord.

We have seen some practical examples of reacting to offense. We have seen that we have a choice in how to react when offense arises, the way of the flesh or God's way. The way of the flesh burdens us, causes stress, and can stunt our growth in the Lord for a time if unforgiveness is present. The way of the Lord removes the burden of offense, brings peace, and allows us liberty to grow into Jesus more effectively. May we choose the Lord's way more and more! Each time an offense arises, we have the opportunity to choose, to learn from Jesus, and to grow. We may fail, but God teaches us through our failures. Remember that we are not determined by our fall but by the rise after the fall. May our Lord Jesus Christ teach us not to be easily offended and train us to be gracious when offense comes! Let us choose God's way and not our way!

LESSON 7 STUDY QUESTIONS

Dealing with Offense

Offenses are something we all deal with as Christian women but don't often discuss. We can carry a burden of offense but never understand how to Biblically deal with it. In this lesson we will practically walk through the steps of how to deal with an offense according to God's Word. As we study this, you may see how you have not followed God's Word properly in the past in regard to offense. Or you may see how others have not followed His Word in regard to you and an offense you have committed in the past. Allow these experiences to teach you. Whether we have made a mistake or someone else has, we can always learn from the missteps. Keep in mind that it is not only our mistakes we can glean from.

1.   How do you think an offense against you should be dealt with? What is your reaction when someone offends you?

2.   Is it right for you to respond this way? Why or why not?

3.   How do you think a person should treat you when you offend her or him?

4.   Is there a difference between the way you treat others when they offend and how you want to be treated when you offend?

We want unmerited favor, grace, and mercy from others when offended. We want to be forgiven in a loving and gracious manner.

But when others offend us, do we respond in the same way? Are we treating them how we want to be treated? Matthew 7:2 says, "For with what judgment you judge, you will be judged; and with the measure you use, it will be measured back to you." May we give out what we want in return. If you judge your brother or sister in Christ, then you will be judged by the same measure. God is a good and just judge. Let Him do His job.

5.   Read Matthew 18:15–17. The next few questions will pertain to this section of scripture. What is the first step in dealing with an offense?

   a) What are you to do if your fellow believer will not hear you the first time?

   b) What do you do if the offending believer will not hear you the second time?

   c) And finally, what do you do if he or she will not hear after the third time?

6.   What might hinder you from approaching someone who has offended you?

7.   How can you benefit from going through this process either as the offended or the offender?

Study Notes

Study Notes

_____

_____

_____

_____

_____

_____

_____

_____

_____

_____

_____

_____

_____

_____

_____

_____

_____

_____

_____

_____

ABOUT THE AUTHOR

Tina is a lover of Jesus. She has been married for twenty years to her best friend, Owen. They have four children, which she homeschools. Owen and Tina enjoy raising children and chickens on their five-acre hobby farm, Wanamaker Farms. They minister together as a family in various capacities. Tina is a chaplain in the local jail, hosts Bible Studies, and speaks at women's events. Tina's heart is to enter into the hard places with women, which she does through discipleship, teaching, writing, and speaking. Her second book, *That I May Know Him*, is available on Amazon as well as other online booksellers.

You can find further teachings and contact the author at tinawanamaker.com.

OTHER WORKS FROM THE AUTHOR

Using life examples and digging deep into God's Word, author Tina Wanamaker inspires her readers with a desire to know Jesus Christ more, to enter into a deeper relationship with God. Full of practical applications of God's Word, this devotional will challenge you to not only talk the talk, but walk the walk. From looking at your foundation upon Christ, to considering what you can learn from trials, to rejecting the lies of the enemy, That I May Know Him will guide you through the ins and outs of daily life from a biblical perspective.

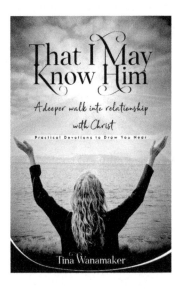

Available on Amazon as well as other online booksellers.

Study Notes

Study Notes

Study Notes

Study Notes

Study Notes

Study Notes

Study Notes

Study Notes

Study Notes

Study Notes